ORACLE

OF THE

COSMIC SPIRITS

Messages From Home

Penny Maier

Foreword by Shelley Kaehr, Ph.D.

Oracle of the Cosmic Spirits   Penny Maier

Oracle of the Cosmic Spirits: Messages From Home

©2011 By Penny Maier

ISBN 10: 0-9648209-8-6

ISBN 13: 978-0-9648209-8-2

Printed in the United States of America

Contact the Author:

Penny Maier

c/o Out of This World® Publishing

PO Box 234

Lewisville, TX 75067

Visit Penny online at
http://www.pennysets.com

Oracle of the Cosmic Spirits   Penny Maier

CONTENTS

Foreword by Shelley Kaehr, Ph.D.   6

Introduction   9

1. CO-CREATOR (USTA)   14
2. LOVING (WAEWA)   16
3. EXPANSION (YOUREL)   18
4. HELLO BODY (ALBAN)   20
5. CHANGE (TREYNON)   22
6. CREATIVITY-FIRE (META)   26
7. MATTER & SPIRIT (VETA)   30
8. SPIRIT OF WATER (WANON)   34
9. EARTH SPIRIT (NON)   36
10. RAINBOW SPIRIT (MYOUS)   38
11. WEB OF LIFE (CELORES)   40
12. CLARITY (KAETO)   42
13. ATOMIC BIRTH (YEWA)   44
14. AS ABOVE-SO-BELOW (TEASO)   46
15. INTEGRATION (JANATA)   48
16. BALANCE (PETONA)   52
17. CONNECTION (ZAYER)   56
18. MANY LIVES (LUM)   58
19. RELATIONSHIPS (NATE)   60
20. VISIONS IN TIME (REMTA)   62

21. SYNTHESIS (OWNLA) 64
22. RENEWAL (NOTAN) 66
23. STEPPING STONES (ANATAO) 70
24. SPIRAL OF LIFE (CRENOUS) 72
25. STAR SEED (TRIA) 74
26. SPHERE (LEATA) 76
27. AIR (ZENONU) 78
28. DISCONNECTION (TON) 80
29. NEW BEGINNINGS (LECIS) 82
30. COMMUNICATION (VETANCA) 84
31. CLARITY OF DREAMS (NAHTA) 86
32. HEART WISDOM (DAYNATA) 88
33. SEEING (AREL) 90
34. LAUGHING (MEATA) 92
35. REMOVAL (JEATO) 94
36. ASCENSION (CEOAT) 96
37. SPARK OF VITALITY (CARNOA) 98
38. NURTURING (BENAE ARREE) 100
39. TRUSTING (UHSA) 102
40. IDEAS (MEACIS) 104
41. GUIDANCE (NEAO) 108
42. DUALITY (RATU) 110
43. UNCONDITIONAL LOVE (CENTAE) 112
44. DANCE OF LIFE (RONU) 114

About the Author 115

ACKNOWLEDGEMENTS

I wish to thank my loving twin flame and husband, Mike for his support and his hard work.

Thanks to all my Earth Angels: Shelley, Julia, Palma, Patti to name just a few.

Thanks to the influences from the other side: Kryon, Abraham, and of course, Aileahna.

FOREWORD

I've been friends with Penny Maier and her husband Mike for several years. We met back in the days when I frequented one of my favorite places, Pensacola, Florida, and they became instructors for my energy healing modality, Galactic Healing.

Since then, Penny and Mike have taken this modality far beyond where I did, and when Penny told me about the special Beings who came to her asking to be pictured so they might be of service to others, without even seeing her drawings, I agreed.

We all receive hunches, feelings, inklings and nudges from beyond the physical world, but are we listening? Not always. I personally believe Beings from other planets and dimensions come to us in hopes to aid us in our journey on earth and that each one of us plays a critical part in moving the planet toward the future.

Oracle of the Cosmic Spirits   Penny Maier

I first experienced the power of these Beings simply by staring at the pictures. Try this and you will find they will light up your neurology. For me, some made my fingers tingle, others brought waves of energy into my forehead. When this happened, I wrote down the number of the photo, then I went back to see what their keynote and message was and found each always represented some stage I was on my path at the time.

You can use this book similarly by opening to random pages, asking Spirit to guide your hand and show you what you need to experience or know at this time. Then go back and read the message.

Or you might turn each page, sense which feels most powerful to you. On first glance you will notice the Beings have similar shapes. This is true, but their energies are very different, all powerful in their own ways.

Oracle of the Cosmic Spirits   Penny Maier

I have a few books on my shelf I turn to daily. *Oracle of the Cosmic Spirits* is among my treasured companions I plan to use for many years to come.

As we approach the imperative changes coming in 2012, more people are opening up to channeling and working with divine energies. Perhaps you are too. I believe the Beings Penny is communicating with will be of assistance and that perhaps by reading their messages, viewing these beautiful photos, you too may open more fully to your divine purpose.

I congratulate Penny for her work with these Beings and for the courage to bring them out into the world at large. I've been working with them ever since she first introduced us, and have received great benefit. I hope you will find the same. Blessings to all who read this!

> Shelley Kaehr, Ph.D.
> Lewisville, TX
> October 21, 2011

Oracle of the Cosmic Spirits   Penny Maier

INTRODUCTION

A short time after being activated to Galactic Healing energies, I began drawing the Beings; the first was Aileahna. I don't know if she is the same Being that brought the healing symbols to our teacher and creator of Galactic Healing (Shelley Kaehr, Ph.D.); but she is a Blue Being. I didn't know who I was drawing, but when I finished, I asked who this was and was told Aileahna. A stream of wonderful Beings came after thereafter. It didn't really hit me that these Beings might be true ethereal energies until one of our friends was having an MRI and saw my Being for Healing around her during the procedure.

It is my belief that these Beings have come forth to help humans with the vibrational expansion and shift. These are heart-centered teachings, which touch your heart and send the vibrations out to the cosmos. Raising our vibration raises Gaia's vibration. The potential is enormous; it all depends on you and what you send out to the universe.

I have included short sayings and intentions for each Being, but we expect you to take their teachings much further. Meditate with each one. Always intend that the information you are given be for your highest good. Ask that the energies sent be at a pace your body can handle. They get excited when you finally ask and want to give too much at once. You are powerful Beings, with unrealized potential. Have fun with the lessons they give you. The earth system is very precious to the cosmos. You are dearly loved for your participation in this Great Experiment.

The Beings are shown in this book in black and white. Some have specific names, which I included. This duality concept gives you a sense of their core energy, the fundamental space from which they emanate.

Oracle of the Cosmic Spirits   Penny Maier

At some point, you may desire a deeper communion with them. This will be possible by visiting our website and seeing them in full color.

Although powerful in the duality form, when viewed in their full colors, their wonderful dance of life expands. These Beings will soon be available in a card deck and as colored prints suitable for framing. This way when you find Beings who you resonate with, you can connect with them further by keeping their image nearby.

You may find some Beings are here to assist you on a temporary basis, while others you will turn to again and again for energy, Spiritual guidance and support.

I wish you peace on your journey with the Beings and that your higher purpose is aided by their presence in your life.

THE BEINGS

Oracle of the Cosmic Spirits   Penny Maier

Co-Creator (USTA)

1 CO-CREATOR (USTA)

Our human form combined with our Spirit creates a co-creator of life. You are invited to embrace your uniqueness. Because you have chosen to live life on Earth, you touch the furthest part of the universe. You are honored for this. What is your soul's life purpose this time? What is your deepest passion? What would you like to crate in your life?

Write it down! Do not say "I want"; say "I choose."

All your thoughts and all your actions affect the furthest reaches of the universe. Go within your heart; feel source pulsating there and be aware of the energy waves that pulse from your heart throughout time and space. You are connected to everything.

Oracle of the Cosmic Spirits   Penny Maier

Loving (WAEWA)

2 LOVING (WAEWA)

You are asked to look into your heart and love who you see. In loving yourself you will be able to love others and life on this wonderful blue planet we call Earth. Love is a hard thing if you have fear and anger in your heart. Let the White light of Spirit enter your heart and wash limitations away. Love is the energy that expands and creates the heavens around us. Your human body can actually create this energy wave called love. Do you see how special that is? Can you see how important you are? Can you sense how special all life is...even the smallest atom?

Oracle of the Cosmic Spirits   Penny Maier

Expansion (YOUREL)

3 EXPANSION (YOUREL)

Spirit is stirring within your heart. Meet the challenge and discover the wonders of universal expansion with "love".

Your life is expanding in many ways. You are evolving, discovering many new ideas and things about yourself that you had no idea you are capable of accomplishing. Believe in yourself; you are a light Being and can accomplish anything you set your mind to do. Connecting with your higher self and Spirit can give you guidance and direction. The path is unfolding before you. Take that first step and begin to see what was there waiting for you all the time.

See the galaxies spiraling within her heart, expanding forever more.

Oracle of the Cosmic Spirits   Penny Maier

Hello Body (ALBAN)

4 HELLO BODY (ALBAN)

This Being represents healing. Something in your life needs healing. It may be a physical healing or it may be an emotional healing.

Go into meditation and work with this Being. Imagine the color of green surrounding you, permeating into you, healing you.

Tell your sacred DNA to activate and heal what you focus on. You know your DNA can do that. If you are a healer, someone will be coming to your for help.

Oracle of the Cosmic Spirits   Penny Maier

Change (TREYNON)

5 CHANGE (TREYNON)

This Spirit embraces the fact of constant change. In our lives, circumstances ebb and flow from day to day. Without change, something sleeps inside of us, yet "the sleeper must awaken."

Be assured, even though we humans may take a step sideways or backwards, the movement is always forward eventually. Staying connected to Source helps life flow smoother.

Let yourself "go with the flow" and relax a little. Ask yourself the following questions:

1) What changes do you need to make?
2) What changes are coming into your life?

Oracle of the Cosmic Spirits   Penny Maier

3) Do you need to let go of some limiting emotions?
4) How can you improve aspects of your life and relationships?

EXERCISE

Seated within this Spirit is a doorway. Find a comfortable place to be still for a moment.

Surround yourself with golden protective light.

Close your eyes and imagine walking through the doorway.

Guidance is waiting if you chose it to be so.

On the following page, write any notes about this experience.

NOTES & MESSAGES FROM THE BEING OF CHANGE

Oracle of the Cosmic Spirits   Penny Maier

Creativity-Fire (META)

6 CREATIVITY-FIRE (META)

This Spirit is all about the energy of creativity. Release that fire within you. You can accomplish your most cherished desires.

This also represents the element of fire. Maybe, you need the addition of fire to balance you or burn an illness out. If you feel there's too much fire, allow water to wash over you.

The energy of the color wavelength of orange allows for the flow of ideas and concepts. The energy of the color

Oracle of the Cosmic Spirits   Penny Maier

wavelength of yellow allows for clarity and organization.

The wavelength of red stimulates action.

Close your eyes. Imagine these colors coming forth from your crown center in the top of your head. Red, Orange, Yellow. Bring each color in one at a time. Notice which colors you need most. Which do you need least? Receive this energy and ask if there are any messages for you. What should you be creating at this time? How can the Being of creativity serve you and assist you in aiding humanity?

NOTES ON CREATIVITY

Oracle of the Cosmic Spirits   Penny Maier

Matter & Spirit (VETA)

7 MATTER & SPIRIT (VETA)

You are asked to bridge the space between matter and Spirit. Your higher self is there waiting to guide you. Can you hear the whispers?

Stand with bare feet touching mother earth; reach your hands to the sky. Visualize your energy field expanding while a white light from the universe comes to meet you.

Feel the light go through your crown. Then imagine the light traveling throughout your whole body, going through your feet to the earth. Seek to raise your

Oracle of the Cosmic Spirits   Penny Maier

vibration. You will begin to hear and maybe even see.

Now open your eyes. What messages did you receive? Write them on the following page.

Oracle of the Cosmic Spirits   Penny Maier

NOTES FROM THE BEING
OF MATTER & SPIRIT

Oracle of the Cosmic Spirits   Penny Maier

Spirit of Water (WANON)

8 SPIRIT OF WATER (WANON)

The earth is 66% water. Your body is mostly water. It has been proven that water properties respond positively to kind and loving words such as: "LOVE AND GRATITUDE."

Do you appreciate the life giving water within you? Do you appreciate the life giving water of the earth? If you have a fear of water, go into meditation with water and ask for the situation to be resolved.

Oracle of the Cosmic Spirits   Penny Maier

Earth Spirit (NON)

9 EARTH SPIRIT (NON)

You are invited to connect back to mother earth. Feel your feet on the life sustaining earth from which your body came. By choosing this Being you may need to set aside some time to reconnect.

Take care of Mother Earth. This is the only home you have. Think of something - no matter how small - that you can start today.

Could you plant a garden? Visit a park? Clean litter from your community? Be creative. Ask the Earth Spirit for guidance.

Oracle of the Cosmic Spirits   Penny Maier

Rainbow Spirit (MYOUS)

10 RAINBOW SPIRIT (MYOUS)

The light we receive from the sun can be broken down into rainbow colors.

Our bodies have colored energy centers that need the light to work properly.

Let the rainbow flow into you, opening and clearing all your chakras. Thank the light that is life giving.

We would not exist on this world without this perfect position from our light source.

Oracle of the Cosmic Spirits   Penny Maier

Web of Life (CELORES)

11 WEB OF LIFE (CELORES)

Embodied in this Spirit is the web of life. We are all connected to each other and the universe.

What you do and say affects everything. Send out hate and you get hate back. Send out love and you get love back.

Which would you like to receive? Our very thoughts and words send out vibrations to all of us on earth and on to the cosmos beyond.

Live as if you are the receiver of everything you put out, because eventually you are.

Oracle of the Cosmic Spirits   Penny Maier

Clarity (KAETO)

12 CLARITY (KAETO)

Imagine this Beings cube to be full of yellow light. The cube helps stabilize. The yellow helps clarity. Clarity will help with forward movement. Mediate with this Being. Imagine going into the cube. Feel the light permeate and resolve unclear issues. Ask your heart if it needs help to clarify the situation. Connect your heart chakra with the solar plexus chakra. Imagine the yellow light and energy of the yellow wavelength passing through each chakra clearing the purpose of each light center. Do you see a clearer path?

Oracle of the Cosmic Spirits   Penny Maier

Atom Birth (YEWA)

13 ATOM-BIRTH (YEWA)

The atom at the heart of this Being represents a creation of a new you.

Remember to acknowledge the very basic building blocks of life. It is here that all things begin and all things can be improved upon, health, love, joy, our very lives. Not only do you have minute atoms and electrons as the foundation of your body, but all things in the universe are made of the same tiny building blocks. They respond to your thoughts.

What will the new you look like?

Oracle of the Cosmic Spirits   Penny Maier

As Above So Below (TEASO)

14 AS ABOVE SO BELOW (TEASO)

The symbol in this Being's heart is two intersecting triangles, representing, "as above-so below." The different shapes of geometric figures resonate to a particular energy, triangular shapes and corners integrate energy. Therefore, the intersecting triangles facilitate connection of our plane of existence with the higher planes. Striving to keep in touch with Spirit is an everyday pleasure. What pleases you most about your connection to Source? Reaching is a start. Touch your heart. Feel the Being within. Would it surprise you to know that Spirit is there also?

Oracle of the Cosmic Spirits   Penny Maier

Integration (JANATA)

15 INTEGRATION (JANATA)

This Being shows a triangle and other patterns brought in to connect with the whole. Thought and energy patterns swell up throughout the Being.

Our whole life is integrated into our essence. This life is added to the many lives we've had through the eons. Our very cells remember.

This Being asks us to remember to integrate the highest vibrations possible. Be discerning what you let filter into your aura and body.

Oracle of the Cosmic Spirits   Penny Maier

Wear your bubble of light as a filter. What are you integrating to make your essence whole?

Did you feel the switch of energy as your eyes traveled from the lower part of the Being to the heart center? Hum!

Record any thoughts or insights on the following page.

Oracle of the Cosmic Spirits   Penny Maier

**NOTES FROM THE
BEING OF INTEGRATION**

Oracle of the Cosmic Spirits   Penny Maier

Balance (PETONA)

16 BALANCE (PETONA)

This Being exhibits two spheres of balance. Balance brings harmony and health to our systems.

When you are drawn to Petona, ask yourself the following questions:

1) Do you need to work on balance in some way?

2) What could you bring into your life that would help you?

Balance is a very complex thing, especially with our complex bodies and our lives.

Oracle of the Cosmic Spirits   Penny Maier

You need to only take one small step to start the process. Just by taking a minute to breathe deeply, you help balance the whole. Chanting or singing brings balance. Drumming and dancing brings balance. Being creative brings balance.

Think of a few of your favorite activities you do to bring balance or ones you would like to do, but haven't yet. What would you like to put on the list? Take a moment now to write down your thoughts.

NOTES ON BALANCE

Oracle of the Cosmic Spirits   Penny Maier

Connection (ZAYER)

17 CONNECTION (ZAYER)

The presence of a cylinder in this Being represents informational connection to Spirit. Understanding comes through the cylinder, integrating through our whole Being. Imagine that cylinder over head, and then listen for the information that is sent to you. Ask that the information be for your highest good. Be ready and the cylinder brings it in quickly. Quieting our mind to be able to hear is very difficult. Do it for a minute, then two. Before you know it, you will be able to still the racing thoughts and hear another voice, bringing forth your many lessons to make a brighter future.

Oracle of the Cosmic Spirits   Penny Maier

Many Lives (LUM)

18 MANY LIVES (LUM)

The soul lives forever. This Being represents the many connecting lives our souls have experienced throughout the universe. Can you remember?

Do you feel there are past lives influencing you now?

You can choose to bring forth the good and leave the bad behind. Bring forth your many lessons to make this go around on earth more productive.

Just ask your cells to start the process. They are waiting for you to direct them.

Oracle of the Cosmic Spirits   Penny Maier

Relationships (NATE)

19 RELATIONSHIPS (NATE)

This Being shows the colors of love and gentleness and joy. By your intention to attract these wonderful attributes in your life partner, you may experience these and much more.

Relationships are complex things. Nurture them and do not take them for granted. The balance of give and take is a dance worth dancing.

Positive intentions are important. Focus on the good attributes you would like to experience from someone.

Oracle of the Cosmic Spirits   Penny Maier

Visions In Time (REMTA)

20 VISIONS IN TIME (REMTA)

We all experience time in this existence. This Being invites you to decide how you will orchestrate your time in this physical world. Take time for yourself. Let time be a measurement of growth and peace and joy. Looking to the past may give insight. Looking to the future helps to prepare. Looking to the here and now helps us to walk forward. Our existence on earth in 3D is measured in time. Did you know there is no linear time when we are back in Spirit on the other side?

Oracle of the Cosmic Spirits   Penny Maier

Syntheses (OWNLA)

21 SYNTHESES (OWNLA)

Connecting body, mind and Spirit is the message of this Being. You have three basic energetic layers that surround your body. The first layer next to the body is connected to physical. The second layer is connected to mental. The third layer is connected to Spirit. When all layers are clear and cohesive, a better state of Being is achieved. Dealing with everyday life may bring hard issues and negative feelings. These collect in your energy field and begin to affect you physically.

Learn to acknowledge the lessons and let go whatever hinders your connection to source. Balance is a hard thing to find. Begin with one tiny thing that makes you feel better, even if it is just sitting outside listening to the birds.

Oracle of the Cosmic Spirits   Penny Maier

Renewal (NOTAN)

22 RENEWAL(NOTAN)

The symbol of infinity is offered by this Being called Renewal.

To meditate with this energy, place your hand on the picture and ask for the universal energy to come into your crown chakra.

Let your heart energy connect with Notan, then form a bubble of golden light around you for protection.

This symbol takes you beyond time and space. Let the energies of the universe renew and heal you, change all that is holding you back to a lesson of truth

enabling forward movement.

There are so many possibilities in your life. Think of the positive, and positive will return to you.

Oracle of the Cosmic Spirits   Penny Maier

NOTES ON RENEWAL

Oracle of the Cosmic Spirits   Penny Maier

Stepping Stones (ANATAO)

Oracle of the Cosmic Spirits   Penny Maier

23 STEPPING STONES (ANATAO)

We experience many stepping stones and paths in our lifetime. Let this path be your heart's desire. Begin today. Notice the little miracles along the way.

Be grateful there is a path to follow. Your path will lead you to many teachers. Take your own truth from them.

Thank them when you are ready to grow again and seek more guidance. You may also be a teacher and mentor for others.

Oracle of the Cosmic Spirits   Penny Maier

Spiral of Life (CRENOUS)

24 SPIRAL OF LIFE (CRENOUS)

The energy of source spirals within us. We are able to create life within us.

New beginnings are coming for you. Be open to new ideas, they might help to create a new you, or ask yourself if there is a new child in your future.

Don't take for granted that you can create. It is a miracle of life. It is absolutely amazing what we are capable of. You are a wonderful light Being.

Oracle of the Cosmic Spirits   Penny Maier

Star Seed (TRIA)

25 STAR SEED (TRIA)

You are the stuff of the universe.

You can become a healer and teacher.

Listen to the Spirits, they will show you the way.

The light Being within us is capable of so much. You have not yet tapped into your true potential.

Allow and trust your higher self to guide you. You have an important role to play in the coming years.

Oracle of the Cosmic Spirits   Penny Maier

Sphere (LEATA)

26 SPHERE (LEATA)

This Being offers a sphere to your consciousness. A sphere means all possibilities-360 degrees.

Enter the sphere and be able to see possibilities you could not see before. Spaces within spaces, time with time, all that is and will be.

Ask to be shown what is for your highest good. Doors will open showing an illuminated path. Are you ready?

Oracle of the Cosmic Spirits   Penny Maier

Spirit of Air (ZENONU)

27 SPIRIT OF AIR (ZENONU)

This Being embodies the air we breathe. Precious air that helps give us life. Feel the wind on your face. The sounds of our breath join the earth and universe. Make each breath count.

Choose to keep this precious air clean and free. Honor air's gift and show gratitude. Still yourself to hear air's wisdom Speak your wisdom to air and let it ride on the wind over the earth and out to the cosmos.

Oracle of the Cosmic Spirits   Penny Maier

Disconnection (TON)

28 DISCONNECTION (TON)

This Being has one wing that seems disconnected, but look closely. It is still connected by the yellow light of Spirit. Let the healing golden light enter your crown and begin to connect and balance your total Being.

You may need to reconnect with life. You may need to connect with someone in your life. Is that someone yourself? Sometimes we may need to go within so our light of Source can shine brighter.

Oracle of the Cosmic Spirits   Penny Maier

New Beginnings (LECIS)

29 NEW BEGINNINGS (LECIS)

This Being wears the green color of spring and healing. May the seeds of your hopes sprout and grow. May the healing you need begin today. Nurture your thoughts and feelings. Experiencing new ideas helps us grow. You will have new teachers come into your life for awhile. New friends, new guides will also come. Isn't it fun to experience the anticipation? A new beginning is coming for mankind. New areas of our DNA will be activated. One can only guess what wonders that will bring!

Oracle of the Cosmic Spirits   Penny Maier

Communication (VETANCA)

Oracle of the Cosmic Spirits   Penny Maier

30 COMMUNICATION (VETANCA)

This Being wears the blue color of communication. Gather your thoughts in order to communicate effectively to others; talk to your guides.

You may hear the answers. Most importantly, speak your truth.

When you speak, you tell the universe what you are and what you are attracting to yourself. Speak wisely. To help the throat chakra work properly, put a blue stone on that area.

Oracle of the Cosmic Spirits   Penny Maier

Clarity of Dreams (NAHTA)

31 CLARITY OF DREAMS (NAHTA)

Some nights we are taught lessons in our sleep.

Dreams may seem cloudy and elusive, but write them down when you wake. Things may become clear and connected later.

What are they trying to work out for you?

Before you sleep, ask to be given clearer pictures and clearer meanings.

Oracle of the Cosmic Spirits   Penny Maier

Heart Wisdom (DAYNATA)

32 HEART WISDOM (DAYNATA)

Listen to your heart and feel the energy from within. Clear that center and connect it with the throat. Then connect with the third eye.

You can now see the heart of the matter and have the wisdom to act. One does not need to be old to have a wise heart. Kindness comes from a wise heart. Caring, loving patience comes from heart wisdom. Our animal friends have heart wisdom as well.

Listen to the messages they give you on your walks. What do they tell you?

Oracle of the Cosmic Spirits   Penny Maier

Seeing (AREL)

33 SEEING (AREL)

What do you see when you look through your eyes? Did you see the bird out your window this morning? Did you see the smile someone gave you for no reason? The Being of Seeing invites you to stop once in awhile and look at the small things that surround you. You will be surprised at what you begin to notice. Now close our eyes. What do you see?

Begin to trust your inner sight. Your higher self will guide you.

Oracle of the Cosmic Spirits   Penny Maier

Laughing (MEATA)

34 LAUGHING (MEATA)

Laughing is a good healer of the emotions. Make someone laugh every day. Seek someone out that makes you laugh.

The positive vibration created when we laugh goes to out to the cosmos.

So…laugh it up!!

Oracle of the Cosmic Spirits   Penny Maier

Removal (JEATO)

35 REMOVAL (JEATO)

This Being sows a corkscrew with an arrow. This symbol can be used to take out unwanted negative energy in our bodies.

Imagine it going in and plucking out imbalance and pain.

It also works in the aura to remove negative thought and dis-ease. Using it in the aura will help prevent sickness from reaching the body.

Ask Jeato to help you to remove anything that is not for your highest good.

Oracle of the Cosmic Spirits   Penny Maier

Ascension (CEOAT)

36 ASCENSION (CEOAT)

Teal is a new color showing up in people's auras. This Being shows the colors of ascension.

We can become more connected to source now with energies changing to higher vibrations.

Allow yourself to relax, to breath and feel the connection. Do you feel the earth's vibrations breathing with you?

Oracle of the Cosmic Spirits   Penny Maier

Spark of Vitality (CARNOA)

37 SPARK OF VITALITY (CARNOA)

This Being's colors speak of vitality, creativity, regeneration. If your body is having an issue with fatigue, bring the colors of orange, red and yellow into your crown chakra. Let the waves of color wash over your whole body then flow out your feet. Maybe there is a project you would like to start or complete. These colors restore your will to continue and also help restore self-esteem and confidence. You are the orchestrator of your own life. See yourself as you wish your life would play out.

Oracle of the Cosmic Spirits   Penny Maier

Nurturing (BENAE ARREE)

38 NURTURING (BENAE ARREE)

This Being reminds you that not only does your soul need nurturing, but your body does as well. Be good to your body. Feed your thoughts as well as your heart. Nurture your children. They will have a very different future than us. Nurture the love of your life. Together you will be stronger. The feeling of nurturing comes from the heart. Did you know that? It is part of the heart wave that extends out forever! Can you imagine what you will be touching? It is almost too grand to conceive, but it is true. You touch the universe with your heart.

Oracle of the Cosmic Spirits   Penny Maier

Trusting (UHSA)

39 TRUSTING (UHSA)

When you rely on gut instinct, that feeling begins in your solar plexus. Trust that instinct and connect it to your heart. Does it say the same thing? Trust in your feelings. Trust in connecting with your higher self. That guidance will never lead you astray. Trust that you are going to know what is the right thing to do in situations. Trust that you are an important part of this plan. Trust in the fact that Source dearly loves you.

Oracle of the Cosmic Spirits   Penny Maier

Ideas (MEACIS)

40 IDEAS (MEACIS)

This Being represents the birth of ideas, they are forming within you. Give them support. Don't dismiss an idea because you think it is not achievable. Believe in yourself! Believe that the universe knows your thoughts and responds to you.

Do you see the blue and purple of Spirit around you, connecting with the thoughts and desires of orange and yellow within you? Be positive in your thoughts and words. The universe will respond in kind. Source may even send an earthly

Oracle of the Cosmic Spirits   Penny Maier

angel to help you and point the way. In the end, it is up to you to bring forth what you wish, but you have many supporters, just ask.

Exercise

Close your eyes now for a moment. Clear your thoughts and allow Source to give you new ideas. What pictures, thoughts or feelings did you come up with?

Jot them down on the following page and call on the Being of Ideas anytime you need special inspiration.

Oracle of the Cosmic Spirits   Penny Maier

NOTES ON IDEAS

Oracle of the Cosmic Spirits   Penny Maier

Guidance (NEAO)

41 GUIDANCE (NEAO)

Gently enveloping you, the blue and purple light of Spirit is offering guidance. Don't dismiss thoughts showing you the way. Don't dismiss a friend showing up just at the right moment.

How about a message from a creature of the forest? Take time to still yourself and listen. Maybe someone needs your council and guidance. Guidance can come in many forms.

Ask and source will arrange to send you those who may illuminate your path.

Oracle of the Cosmic Spirits   Penny Maier

Duality (RATU)

42 DUALITY (RATU)

There is yin and yang in all creation.

You may need to balance forces in your life.

Bring the two-diamond window together matching them perfectly.

As the two diamonds connect, life force energy burst forth illuminating you in golden light. Slowly take yourself into the diamond window.

Your answers may be there, a guide may be there waiting for you. Are you ready to see and hear?

Oracle of the Cosmic Spirits   Penny Maier

Unconditional Love (CENTAE)

43 UNCONDITIONAL LOVE (CENTAE)

This is Ilea. Notice the light of Source spiraling within her heart. The energy that unconditional love produces is what expands the universal planes and creates life.

Our existence in this plane sometimes makes it difficult to achieve an unconditional state of mind and heart. The connection is worth striving for however, because it raises our vibrations as well as earth's vibrations.

Have you heard the expression "love can move mountains?"

Oracle of the Cosmic Spirits   Penny Maier

Innately we know love is a powerful emotion. Meditate with Ilea.

Imagine the golden light of the universe spiraling out to encompass you in light and love. Imagine a spiral within your heart. Let it spiral out to the universe.

Allow Spirit to send love to you. You can also imagine the wave of light and love going to someone who needs a little encouragement.

Oracle of the Cosmic Spirits   Penny Maier

44 DANCE OF LIFE (RONU)

The Being on the cover of this book is called Dance of Life. This Spirit reminds you that life is a wonderful dance.

Appreciate the wonderful things in life. Do you see joy coming from Spirit? You are the dancer and choreographer of this moment in time. Participating in life is your main purpose each time you come back to Gaia. Yes, you scheduled some main events and lessons, but ultimately you have free will.

Maybe, you are hesitating because the next step is an unknown. Imagine yourself floating within the spiral of this

Oracle of the Cosmic Spirits   Penny Maier

Being's heart. Ask your higher self to give you help with this decision. Connect your heart with the spiral and let the information flow from the spiral energy to your consciousness.

When you are ready, let the energy flow back to your heart. Release the energy to the universe.

Source knows your intentions now. Your intentions will be matched with in kind energy. May you always dance!

Oracle of the Cosmic Spirits   Penny Maier

Dance of Life (RONU)

ABOUT THE AUTHOR

Penny Maier grew up in Albuquerque, New Mexico. She began drawing outlines of these Beings when she was a teenager. The Beings were trying to communicate then, but she didn't know the significance of her random doodles. She began to awaken in the late 1990's. At that time she began to have healing energy pour out of her palms. In 2008, she began to draw these energies that have become the *Oracle of the Cosmic Beings*. Only in 2011, did she realize that even though she had become a healer, her main mission was to send the energy of these Beings out to the world. It is her hope that they will illuminate the path for those that connect with their energies.

Visit her online at
http://www.pennysets.com